Messages
FOR OUR

Daughters

10 Week Challenge

#SelfiEVAL
#QueensBE

Shonakiki P.

SAVELIZ PRESS

Messages For Our Daughters

10 Week Challenge #SelfiEVAL #QueensBE

PUBLISHED BY SAVELIZ PRESS

ISBN 978-0692493496
ISBN 0692493492

In my mind, I had already begun brainstorming the contents of my "Masterpiece Book" which was in a completely different direction than this book. I was in full preparation mode for a work I thought and still think worthy to be shared. Then one day I sat down with my little black notebook in hand and began to write. As I laid words to paper I suddenly realized I had taken a detour I had no intentions of taking. I detoured but I was not lost. I found myself sharing to those who were born queens to be in their own right. I was sharing messages to my miracle daughters; they were messages about God and messages about life.

Later given the assignment to share them with you, these writings were penned from the heart as a call to your hearts. They are a journey of self evaluation. It is my hope that you will carefully read the message each week; do the work of each challenge, and journal your thoughts along the way. When the challenge seems difficult continue to push through. There is a method to the madness. You will be encouraged. You will be inspired. You will be challenged. You will have your brief encounter with the Queen God has destined you to be.

Therefore, to any young lady whose mind, heart, and spirit are up to the challenge for the next 10 weeks…come, sojourn with me.

ACKNOWLEDGMENTS

To my beautiful miracle babies Layla E., RiRi, and April, I thought God entrusted me to raise you, love on you, and protect you while here on this earth. However, I realized your presences in my life were purposed for far more than that. The essence of your being stopped me from being. It stopped me from being so afraid of living. It would not allow me to be content being selfish with my love. Yes. It was your essence that stopped me from being and allowed me to BE. I am sure I speak for many mothers when I say because of you daughters, our love has catapulted to new levels unlike any we have ever known. Our meters of compassion, since your birth, have gone far past the point of no return.

God poured into me through you. Now allow me to pour back into you and others through lessons I have learned while following Him.

To my amazing, hard working husband, I thank you for supporting me and impelling me to walk in my destiny. Thank you for being a praying man. I love you.

Find Your Light; Be The Light

Week 1

"Your beauty should not come from outward adornment, such as elaborate hairstyles and the wearing of gold jewelry or fine clothes. Rather, it should be that of your inner self, the unfading beauty of a gentle and quiet spirit, which is of great worth in God's sight."

1 Peter 3:3-4 NIV

To my daughters, my future queens, I say to you examine yourselves daily to become a better person. In these times our world has experienced changes that offer you, my sweet innocents, no substance of quality. Instead you are greeted daily with a vast amount of meaningless -- dare I say it-- garbage that weakens the beautiful light you were born with day by day. You see, it's not enough in this 21st century to walk out of your front door adorned with an inner beauty that shines so bright not even death could extinguish it. *I know death is pretty harsh to think about but that's how bright I think our lights should be; be so bright that your shine will last long after you are gone.*

Our reality today is that Reality T.V. has become the vision board for many of your delicate futures. It constantly glamorizes all of the things that beauty is surely not. Ill behavior, fake hair, fake breasts, fake buttocks, fake nails, illusions of "flawless" faces that are carefully, yet overly painted and too many other things to name; these are all distractions from seeing the real you. God created us all with our very own flaws to stand out in a crowd. So when you adorn yourself in the same distractions as everyone else then you become just as everyone else…common and lost in the crowd of lookalikes. You no longer shine brighter than the brightest diamond.

When we focus much of our time and energy on looking good physically, we unintentionally take the focus away from enhancing our inner beauty. To look in a mirror and be just as pleased with the "bare boned" beauty staring back at you is far greater than any over exaggerated physical attribute. ***What good are shiny and pretty material things when the soul of a woman is poorly lit?*** All queens have purpose yet purpose can never be found when one is lost in a sea of worldly treasures. When all of those treasures become lost, or tarnished, or mangled, or faded, or worn, what then is left?

Though I have many more things to learn I now know that the gentleness of the soul is what makes others feel moved by its presence. It is what gives hope many times without even knowing hope is needed. It gives light. It lends love. It shares pain. It is the one thing that gives us all the SUPER power to be able to reach deep into the hearts of others to help heal hurts and soothe pain. Truth? Unlike our society's highly praised false beauty, a gentle soul doesn't even need to be physically present *to be present*. Now that, my dears, is a powerful form of beauty.

Week 1 Challenge:

1. This day pick two of your closest friends or a family member, such as a mom, brother, sister, or father and ask them for help by sharing their honest opinion with you. Have two to three people write their honest opinion of you on a small note. How do they see you today? Don't get offended if the note has something in it that you would disagree with. Let's face it, there is no perfect person. Once you have received each of the letters it is okay to take a look at them but once you've done that place them in a little lock box, dresser drawer, or location that you can go back to at the end of this 10 week "SelfiEVAL" project and pull them out for a later review.

2. The only way we grow in life is by taking self evaluations, listening, learning, and making a conscious effort to be better than we were the day before. This second part of week one challenge requires you to peel off all of your make-up, eye shadows, blushes, and lipstick. You will continue the remainder of this 10 week challenge without these enhancements.

3. Take a washable window crayon (or a sticky note) and write your favorite short positive saying on the mirror that you look at every day. Here are a few examples:

I am BEAUTIFUL
Dear Self, today you will love beyond comfort!

Journal your Week 1 thoughts on the following page.

(If you have social media accounts and you choose to share pieces of your self evaluation journey please be sure to use the hashtags below.)

#MessagesForOurDaughters
#SelfiEVal
#QueensBE

Weekly Chronicle:

_____

_____

_____

_____

_____

_____

_____

#SelfiE-VAL   #QueensBE

8

Be of Service

Week 2

"Not looking to your own interests but each of you to the interests of the others."

Philippians 2:4 NIV

Have you ever stood by and watched a girl be ridiculed? Have you ever noticed the girl who always walks alone and eats alone yet she has the most genuine "hello" out of all the pretty girls you know? Though alone, she always stands out in a crowd to you. She's not noticed by everyone but she's noticed by you. Others say she's not the most pretty yet she possesses an alluring beauty that speaks to you through the humility in her eyes. Ever wondered why this girl was one of the most popular, unpopular girls in your world? Could it be that you are the being that could speak life into her world?

You, my Princesses, should know that every one you meet is fighting or has fought some sort of battle. Many times those battles are unseen to the naked eye. Therefore, because her smile is still so soft after the ridicule and her mannerisms seem to be without bitterness does not mean she doesn't suffer inside. Many girls are taught to be strong and to hold their head high despite any adversity they may be facing. They are taught to disguise it; hide it. All the while, their souls are screaming for a kindred spirit to share both pains and celebrations with them. So in that moment when you notice her being mistreated by others, do you step in to shoo away the offenders on her behalf?

You should always be interested in the lives of others. *--no, I don't mean finding the most juicy of juice to gossip about either--* Concern yourself with helping others or serving others. Over the years I have found that one of the most rewarding feelings comes from being of service to others. Your service to her could be as simple as putting into place that patch of hair that has gone astray on her head, stubbornly standing away from the rest of her hairs. It could be the shooing away of her hagglers. There is no required weight standard for a good deed. No such scale has ever existed. Therefore, being of service to someone else should never be about how grand the tangible is and it should NEVER be broadcasted to an audience in hopes to receive accolades. You see my loves the moment you have to tell someone about your great well doing is the moment that your pride takes center stage and your kind act of service is all but diminished to be nothing more than a simple act.

Far too many radiant daughters of God are dimming their own lights because they feel they are alone and their problems will never end. I would have you to always remember a Queen does not become who she is by living shallow and there is nothing more shallow than being concerned about only you. So I ask you. The next time you see that girl in any form of distress what will you do?

Week 2 Challenge:

1.   This week I would have you to be aware of everyone around you. Try leaving an anonymous note that will uplift the spirits of whoever will behold its contents. Share your favorite motivational quote or simply share with them the great thing you've noticed about them. Spend this week uplifting other young ladies and spreading joy.

2.   This week you are also challenged to go out into your community and do something for the less fortunate no matter how small or big.

Journal your thoughts for Week 2 on the following page.

Weekly Chronicle:

_____

_____

_____

_____

_____

_____

_____

#SelfiE-VAL   #QueensBE

Prayer Life

Week 3

"Being confident of this, that he who began a good work in you will carry it on to completion until the day of Christ Jesus."

Philippians 1:6 NIV

My loves, have you ever had your heart set on accomplishing a goal but you were too afraid to take the first step necessary to accomplish it? Why do you think that is? One of my favorite quotes is "Fear is the thief of all dreams" by Brian Krans. Please know when you plug in to God's word you will begin to understand there is no reason to ever fear man or the rejection of man. Fear can stifle your life. It can cause you to bottle up all of your ambitions and store them deep within the quiet parts of your soul never to be shared with the world. For every one of you that suppresses your dream because of fear you take from us that extra glimmer of light that only you can give. I write to tell you there should be nothing or no one worthy of obtaining power because of your fear. It was told to me once when I was a little girl that *every man and woman I will face in life gets up in the morning and puts on their pants one leg at a time…JUST. LIKE. ME.* So why fear them? *--of course my mom pumped me up with that one. Thank you Doris!--*

I could also recall the days when I was a young girl and I would fear something or I would experience pain because of something. My mother would always talk about prayer. She helped to plant the seed in my siblings and me that prayer would help us through anything. She would tell us to turn to Psalms 91 in the Bible and read it whenever we were afraid. Psalms 23 was also a favorite of hers. While I did not yet fully understand the power of prayer I would heed her advice and pray about my situations anyway. It is important that you know God already knows the things we need before we ourselves even know. He knows of our wants; he knows our heart's most deep desires. What He wants from us is that we seek Him with our whole hearts. Whether it be in our brightest of days or our darkest nights, we should always pray and seek the council of God in every aspect of our lives.

For when we pray and connect with God we lay our foundation of strength prayer by prayer. It is the strength needed that will help you carry on with a smile on your face when you experience your first heart break. It is the strength that will give you comfort when you experience the pain of loss. *"We can rejoice, too, when we run into problems and trials, for we know that they help us develop endurance." Romans 5:3*

While some of you may feel comfortable in making prayer an intricate part of your life, others are not. Some of you may feel like you don't know how to pray. Some of you may be even ashamed to pray in front of others. There is no need to be ashamed so please kindly erase the thought of a perfect prayer from your mind. Everyone prays different prayers because everyone is living a different life with different needs and wants. In prayer you talk to HIM. Do so just as you would with your parents. I tell you there is so much peace and comfort you will find when you choose to pray. I could recall my days of being in school and getting ready for a big test. I would almost always say a quick prayer at my desk just after the teacher would begin the quiz. It would always calm my anxiety and fear of the test. You must know that every problem you encounter in life is cause for prayer and every good day you manage to shake a tail feather with in life is cause for prayer. It does not matter if it is a prayer of thanks, one of supplication, one on behalf of someone else, one for confessing or one of reverence.
--Grab the dictionary for supplication and reverence if you are unsure--
Every single moment within every single day of your life is cause of prayer.

Week 3 Challenge

1. So, now that we've gotten that out of the way what are the first set of goals/fears you're planning to conquer? I am sure you have heard others say write the vision and make it plain. It really does help to see your goals written and in plain view. There you will have your constant reminder of why you must push through your obstacles when they become present in your life. What career path are you planning to take in the future? Write down 5 short term goals that will help get you one step closer to where you want to be. Within the next 30 days work hard

on bringing at least one of those goals to completion. Mark them off your list as you complete them. Be sure to ask God in prayer to guide you on the path you seek if it is his will.

2. This week I would also have you to begin focusing on your prayer life. *--you can NEVER be too young to have a strong prayer life--* If you are used to saying the traditional prayer that begins with "Our Father, who art in heaven…" that is perfectly okay. You can say that prayer to completion and add unto it. Take your time and talk with God during your prayer. Talk with Him about how your day went. Don't be afraid to give him praise because he wakes you up daily and gives you another chance to share your beautiful self with the world. The biggest challenge with prayer for the next 7 weeks is to say grace at dinner or lunch time for the family at least once a week. Hold hands around the dinner table or where ever you all may be partaking in dinner and say a prayer of thankfulness (grace) on behalf of everyone there. Be sure to journal your feelings of this experience.

3. This week you will peel off the layer of any enhancements you have added unto the natural you to serve as an extension of you. This will include hair, lashes, fake eyes, nails etc. You will remain without any of these enhancements for the next 7 weeks. *--trust me, there's a method to this madness--* Now peel.

Journal your week 3 thoughts on the following page.

Weekly Chronicle:

_____

_____

_____

_____

_____

_____

#SelfiE-VAL   #QueensBE

Pruning the Spirit

Week 4

"Finally brothers and sisters, whatever is true, whatever is noble, whatever is right, whatever is pure, whatever is lovely, whatever is admirable-if anything is excellent or praiseworthy-think about such things."

Philippians 4:8 NIV

It is true what they say, what your mind conceives you become. Confession time for this mom **said as I hang my head in shame****. I began indulging in reality television some years ago and found myself intrigued with peeking into the lives of others. This was before reality t.v. became the platform for rebirthing careers of many celebrities or jump starting careers for those who have an uncontrollable thirst for fame. I was unaware that while I, in my true reality form, was weeding drama out of my life I was simultaneously still supping on drama at least once or twice a week via the television. My urge to view scenes showing people fighting one another or acting in a behavior unbecoming increased. I would replay those scenes over and over in my own head on how I would handle the on-screen situations if I were a part of them. Sadly, I must admit, in my thoughts I almost never took the peaceful route. How many of you do that now?

My future queens, while your minds are still so young and your mistakes are few you must learn to guard your thoughts. ***By default, our nature as a flawed human being is easier to be misguided and led toward negative things than it is toward positive things***. Do you believe that? We are sinful by nature so we must make a constant effort to water our spiritual garden in hopes to bear fruits of purity and love. Because we are in the age of social status, your mental space can be easily clouded with junk from both the media and people who are not truly people you would spend your time with in public. Why wouldn't you?

16

You would not do so because you know they bring with them madness of all kinds. I must say girls, there is hope for you having a loving cyber space. However it is up to you to make it so. Just as you can steer clear of being in the physical company of people who have no respect of your walk with Christ, so can you in your cyber space.

For the sake of this message let us all put on our make believe overalls and big farmer hats. We have some tilling to do! Your social media is like your cyber garden. Today you will remove all of the unclean people and pages that taint your online space. Secondly, begin adding unto your personal library within your home. We must read more things of value like the Bible and other inspirational books and turn off tubes. Try finding a Bible Study group and become a regular there. Find a favorite motivational website and bookmark it on your mobile device. Make it your mission to take the light with you everywhere you go. Consume its rich contents and get tipsy from it on a daily basis. You must surround yourselves with positive things along with positive like-minded people and feed off of one another as you seek a higher level in Christ.

Truth is... God sent his only son to die for our sins. Truth is God deserves a praise not only for every blessing but for every tough lesson HE allows you to go though. Truth is *--for all of the naysayers--* social media can be a wonderful tool as long as you do yourself a service and clean house regularly. Fill your life with Christ-like, loving thoughts and you will find that you will never need validation from people but rather gain a craving to receive affirmations from God. Good day my future queens. Think on things pure. Think on things positive. Think on all good things. Now make your way to your social media accounts today *--if you have one--* and let's clean house!

Week 4 Challenge:

1. This week, for those of you that have one, search for a minimum of three great social media accounts that could be beneficial to your well-being and plug in to them. You must have at least three by week's end. For those of you with no social media accounts, add another or purchase your very first book filled with inspiration. Begin building your library of life. Remember, as you are living out your days you are also writing your history. Be inspired. Be encouraged. #QueensBE

2. Review your friend's list and begin deleting any account that is filled with negativity, obscene things, or hate.

Journal your thoughts for Week 4 on the following page.

Weekly Chronicle:

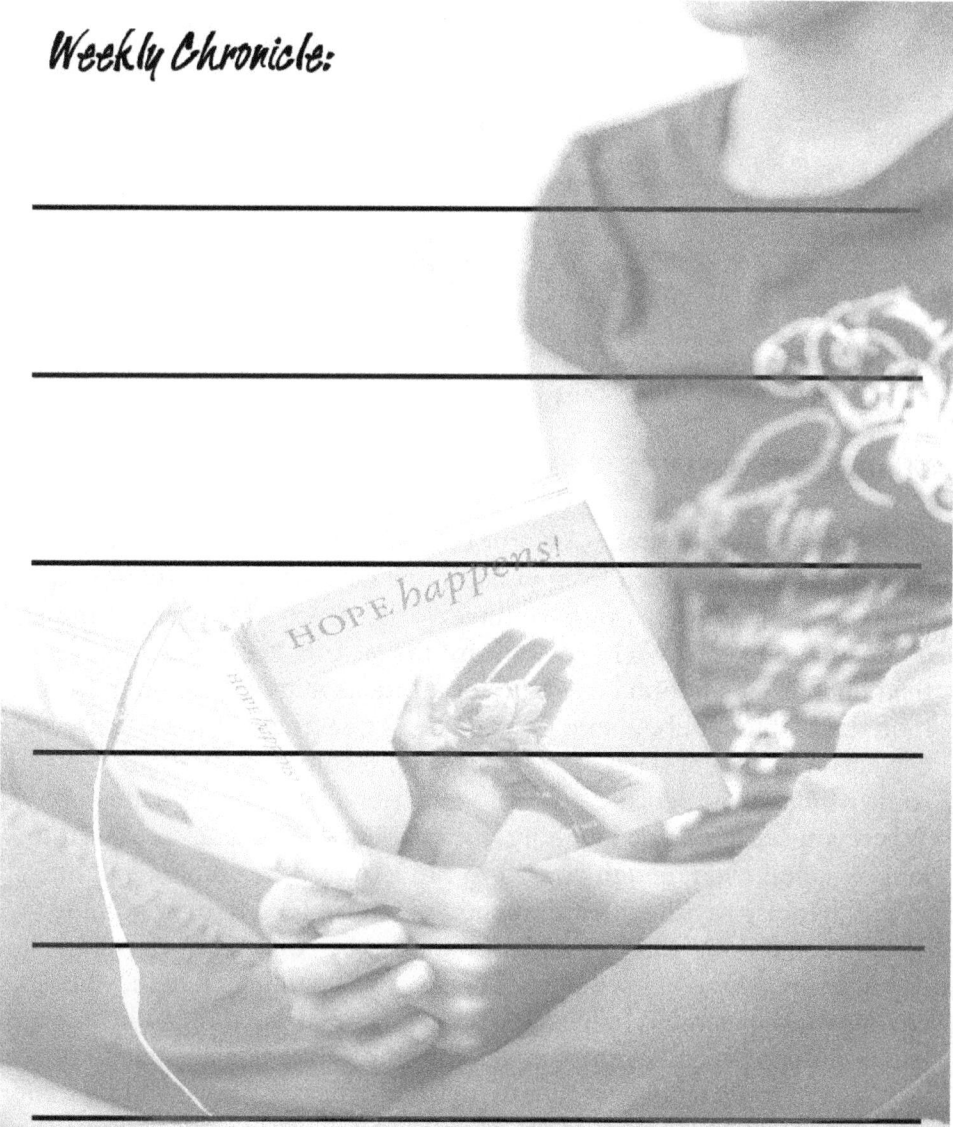

_____

_____

_____

_____

_____

_____

#SelfiE-VAL   #QueensBE

#CheckYourself

WEEK 5

"A good man brings good things out of the good stored up in him, and an evil man brings evil things out of the evil stored up in him."

Matthew 12:35 NIV

As young ladies of immense worth I say to you never allow your existence to be devalued by anyone. Some day *--if not already--* you may find yourself in a swarm of mean girls. Always be aware of the company you keep. We have all heard the saying, "One bad apple spoils the bunch". This notion rings true for attitudes and people. Let's take a moment and think about emotions. When your friend is sad you are sad, correct? When your friend feels angry about something you too feel some of that anger, correct? When your friend is happy, you are happy. When you see someone laughing uncontrollably, it makes you want to laugh as well even though you don't fully know why you are laughing. We all happily say laughter is infectious but we tend to overlook the actuality that both behavior and attitude can be contagious as well.

I hear my daughters sometimes discussing the things that they've encountered in school. I am so baffled at some of the things I hear because I don't recall ever experiencing things like that at such a young age. I went to their school recently to drop off one of my daughters after she had just had her arm casted. The reason for the cast is another conversation. *--Let's just say gymnastics scarred me for sure!* -- I went to the school and the first person I engaged was one of the little cast minion's (my youngest daughter) teachers. After a very brief greeting, the teacher immediately began telling me about how jealous one of the little girls in the class was of my daughter. The girl would always have negative remarks because she did not like the idea of my daughter being confident about her intellect in class. Just as I have always ensured that her father and I instill the importance of humility in her, we also do our best to instill confidence. While the news was not new to me because I talk to my daughters daily after school about school, I was still quite shocked. I was a bit taken aback due to hearing it from the teacher because at that point it was surely clear to me what my daughter might have been experiencing at school was deeper than I'd thought. Mean girls were swarming.

Young ladies, I want you to always, always take self-inventory. Even when you feel in your heart that you are a good person you should still CHECK yourself regularly. I don't want you to become one of those women who spend their days despising the existence of another simply because you have allowed yourself to feel inferior to her. ***The moment that you become comfortable in the idea that you are such a good person with a good heart is the moment you make the decision to fail at being the best person you can be according to God's word.*** You must guard your thoughts often to keep focused doing the right things.

You see my darling, when you check yourself on the regular you will find yourself living a life of richness in mental health. When your thoughts are not consumed with little whispers about the lives of others there is a lesser chance of you being distracted from concentrating on your future successes. Never be the one to disseminate the gossip. Do not be a whisperer of the whispers unless you are doing so for the liberation of another and be attentive of where your loyalty lies. --*You could be an accessory to bullying and not even know it*-- Have you ever had a friend that wanted you to be angry with someone because he or she is angry with that person? You've never had any problem with the person they want you to be angry with but they will not consider you a good friend or loyal because you choose to not be angry. Take a few minutes and think on this one thing. When judgment day comes which do you think God will say?

"Well done my child. You showed extreme courage and loyalty to your friend. You were angry with, showed ill-will toward, and were hateful to another child of mine. You chose to behave in the manner because your friend had a disagreement with them".

"Well done my child, you showed so much grace and love to the enemy of your best friend despite what the two of them were going through. You were such an example of my grace. You unknowingly

21

served as the guide that helped the two of them move past their issue and into a better place."

The issue at hand will be about how you made the decision to mistreat or be mean to someone just because they are enemies of your "EARTHLY" friend or to love someone in spite of. If you should ever find yourself in a situation such as this, set your sights on being the voice of reason. Sprinkle a little of your positive sparkle into the lives of two people rather than teaming up with one and injecting negativity into the life of the other. Therefore as a child of God, the princess of our King who'll someday be a Queen, I ask you to whom do your loyalties lie? Your answer here: _____

Ecclesiastes 4:9-10 *"Two are better than one, because they have a good return for their labor: If either of them falls down, one can help the other up. But pity anyone who falls and has no one to help them up."* Always #CheckYourself but be ready to #CheckAFriend too should the need arise.

Week 5 challenge:

1. This week I want you to have an open and honest discussion with your friend or group of friends about loyalty. Many times friendships are broken because of the misconception of loyalty. The goal of this challenge is not to force someone to change their mind about the issue but rather be a source of enlightenment. The goal is simply to highlight each of your perceptions of loyalty in hopes that it does not become a negative factor in your relationship later in life.

2. This week there will be no peeling. You will be adding. For the next 5 weeks, you will enhance your wardrobe so that all of your sacred parts will be covered modestly. This means no tight shirts that will sound the alarm for all to see the curves of your breasts. No tight pants or jeans. If that is all you have, wear a shirt that has length in the back and will cover the buttocks area. Skirts that flow are also a great choice. You're young. Be creative! When you take the attention off of your body, you immediately add more value to yourself and the world's perception of you. Ever seen someone dressed in a manner that showcased every

curve they had? They showcase curves but still complain about how young men hound them and disrespect them. Don't be that one.

Journal your Week 5 thoughts on the following page.

Weekly Chronicle:

_____

_____

_____

_____

_____

_____

_____

#SelfiE-VAL   #QueensBE

24

Competition and Envy

WEEK 6

"The sun has one kind of splendor, the moon another and the stars another; and star differs from star in splendor."

1 Corinthians 15:41 NIV

I say to you my loves you are a gift to this world. What you possess in the make-up of your unique beauty, no one else in this world has. You have a smile that is meant to light up someone's world and a touch that will one day serve as a safe haven for the one who will find comfort in your hugs.

Sometimes our senses become overwhelmed as we sit on the outside looking into the windows of others lives swooning over all of the "wonderful" material things they have. We see and listen to others sing the praises of those people so much until it begins to be the force that shifts our thoughts from being content with what we already have to thirsting for more. As you journey through this life you will find there are others out there who live their lives hoping for the downfall of someone else because they do not like seeing anyone have more than them. It is my prayer that you never become one of those women.

Please understand we can all be great together but in our very own light. It is not meant for one person to have it all. You see a Queen knows that it is impossible for her to have it all while the ladies of her court possess nothing. A Queen knows that each woman carries with her a quality that makes her stand apart from everyone else. However, collectively she and the ladies of the court have a presence so powerful it sends a message of love, loyalty, and support loudly to anyone who stands in their company. A Queen…she is who she is with or without all of the gold. A Queen…she knows how to rejoice with others when they've found their light.

Therefore, to you princesses, please know that inner peace and joy surpasses all material things. It is that inner peace and joy that will have you content and extremely happy in life with what you have. It will separate you from the rest of the pack; It'll give you that one special kind of jewel that was made specifically for your crown. You see I didn't grow up in a rich home but when I walked through the doors every day I felt like I was stepping into an indoor oasis. There was never a need for me to want what anyone else had or to be jealous of someone else's blessings. It is not about how grand something is in size but rather how grand the contents are that can be found within it. It's not about how much something costs but about the impact that it makes when it is felt or looked upon. You, my dear have to embrace every season you enter into. It is then that you will learn the lessons designed specifically for your life.

To the souls that are lost, struggling, and feel your big amazing life is small and boring, be encouraged. Stop comparing your life to what is perceived to be grand things in the lives of others. For when you compare, you bring about envy...jealousy. Understand that we are not all meant to have and do the same things. You just remain humble and take care of all that God has blessed you with. Understand that it is better to be rich in the intangible things. Choose to be happy. ***Be you on purpose every day. Don't change to appeal to anyone. Be YOUR absolute truth. JUST. BE. YOU.***

Week 6 Challenge:

1. Today you will peel off all jewelry and bling for the remainder of this 10 week SelfiE-VAL project. You must only adorn yourself with your beautiful smile and your genuine, sweet spirit. p.s. *A smile is always in fashion.*

Journal your Week 6 thoughts on the following page.

Weekly Chronicle:

_____

_____

_____

_____

_____

_____

_____

#SelfiE-VAL   #QueensBE

Calm the Spirit

WEEK 7

"My dear brothers and sisters, take note of this: Everyone should be quick to listen, slow to speak and slow to become angry, because human anger does not produce the righteousness that God desires."

James 1:19-20 NIV

Words thrown about out of anger are like a multitude of daggers. They are positioned to pierce the heart in all of the right places with a plan to shed blood for all of the wrong reasons. Anger is usually the result of two people not being able to communicate with one another in a manner that would be successful for all involved. As you grow older you will find yourself being faced with many different changes in your life. Some will bring with them pain packaged in the most beautiful way. It would be like opening a jack in the box with the revealing of the box's contents being less than appealing. It is that pain that will cause the gentle spirit you were born with to waiver and straddle the lines of standing strong despite your hurt or giving in and becoming one quick to speak out of anger because you will have allowed it to control you.

Sidetracking a little bit here but wanted to share. This afternoon I overheard a conversation between my two daughters about a book. One daughter asked the other how could she read books like The Book Thief or The Life of Pi for example because those books were --in her words-- BORING! She went on to say that she'd rather read books that are going to help her get through life. I secretly smiled immensely as she continued on saying how unruly so many of the children were that she'd recently come in contact with during her school day. I thought to myself...this is exactly why I'm writing. Despite all of the negative darkness surrounding you all today there are still some of you that want better. This is why I have chosen to put these tidbits of messages within

28

these pages for you. I just love confirmations. Now back to what I was saying.

As I have told my daughters many times, I share with you as well. Stay in communication with God and the word because the more you fill your spirit with HIM, the more joy and peace you will be filled with. Joy is truly a wrangler of anger. Because one possesses joy, the likelihood of exhibiting irrational behavior because of madness is little to none. There may be a time when you are pushed to an anger so heavy that it causes you to cry. The cry is not because you are weak but because you are putting up such a fight with your flesh to refrain from violence. Now, that my darlings is not irrational behavior but can be seen as a form of strength. It also shows that you are in control of your actions and mindful of doing things God's way. Don't ever let anyone tell you differently. If you find that you are ever pushed to those lengths choose to walk away. Walk away when angry and only return to confront the matter when you have prayed about the issue and are calm.

Though some may beg to differ, know that it is absolutely okay to break down and cry. -- E*ven I still get a good cry in every now and again* -- Have your moment but be ready to step back into your glory and carry on with the divine life God has blessed you with. No matter how bad your day is or how many people hurt you along the way, it is God's love that will help you stay strong. Allow His love to paint your days yellow when it seems that your entire world is colored red. **Because you are God's child, know that YOU are love and you ARE loved.**

Week 7 Challenge:

1. This week you will create a quick ditty that you can use at the onset of your anger should it find you. You can simply use one word. Mine… #MERCY. While it does not stop the anger all of the time, if I say it a few times the initial spark of my anger will catch its wind and weaken a bit before my response. Therefore, instead of trying to extinguish a raging blaze all at once, I then only have to be concerned with diminishing the life of a burning flame that has been sedated by my ditty. I'd rather deal with the outcome of the latter of the two. Wouldn't you?

Journal your Week 7 thoughts on the following page.

Weekly Chronicle:

_____

_____

_____

_____

_____

_____

_____

#SelfiE-VAL   #QueensBE

Temptations; Reserves; Your Temple

WEEK 8
PART I

"And lead us not into temptation, but deliver us from the evil one."

Matthew 6:13 NIV

Good day to you my beautiful future queens. It is now week 8 of this self evaluation journey. Today I am going to talk about something that - *in most cases*- scares the heebie jeebies out of parents. --*Yes, I know great choice of words*-- To all of us parents you are our precious jewels, our queens to be...some of our most prized possessions. We sometimes worry about the things you could possibly be tempted with so today I chose to touch on TEMPTATION. First things first...temptation is not of God but it is allowed by God. It can creep up on you like the sun that rises for the breaking of day, swift and incognito. As children of God naturally we find ourselves struggling at times to make the right decisions especially when we know right from wrong. *"Anyone who knows the right thing to do, but does not do it, is sinning." James 4:17.*

My daughters tell me all the time about the young boys and girls in the school that spend their day aimlessly trying to figure out who likes who and carelessly trading germs via the mouth by the hall lockers. So I say to you, while temptation may come in many different areas of life I'd prefer to relate it to youth dating and relationships for the sake of these writings. Many of the young children at my daughters' school are all into dating but they lack the knowledge of knowing what dating should really be all about. Is it about finding someone to hold hands with? Is it about doing what everyone else is doing when it comes to having a boyfriend? Is it about getting a high off of the puppy love and having a partner to -- *dare I say it* --experience sex with? One of the biggest issues I know many of you may face today or may face in the near future is making the decision to start dating and also exploring the idea to partake in sexual activities.

My loves, having sex out of wedlock is a sin. Of course not because I said so, but biblically the idea is frowned upon. It is called fornicating for those of you that did not know. I want you to ask yourself a question. Take out a pen and a piece of paper and write this question at the top of the page just as the following sentence is written. "What are the top three benefits of dating at such a young age in regards to me becoming successful and finding my purpose in life?" Once you have written it you can then answer it. If you cannot think of a fair-minded answer then allow me to answer the question for you. There are no benefits and it most certainly will not help you find your purpose in this lifetime. Therefore, keep in mind while we are not perfect let us all still make every effort to not fall prey to temptation and sin.

Did you know that the simple holding of one's hand could stir up feelings between two people that otherwise may have never been felt? Ask any parent and they will tell you that dating leads to holding hands, which leads to hugging, then kissing, and finally the discovery of the perfect place to privately get intimate with one another. Once those feelings are stirred that is when temptation starts tugging at your will with no intentions of letting go until you give in. It also rears its ugly head when peer pressure arrives at the lunch table as you are surrounded by friends or others who have already crossed the line by entering into that *restricted zone*. It sometimes silently coaxes you aggressively into doing what everyone else is doing. In the process you fall in love with a young boy whom you don't truly know because he is just a boy. He, himself doesn't know who he is in his youthful years. Not to mention you are also still learning who you are. So this leads me back to the question I had earlier but presented to you in a different way. Why do you date or feel the need to date?

Though I gave you a brief pause in the reading to answer this question earlier, here is an opportunity to think on these things longer. Between now and beginning to read Part II of this week's message, please write a list of reasons you feel dating is beneficial and what purpose it would serve you in your young years as you find yourself in this life's journey. I am going to pause the writing at this point and continue with Part 2 *--the meat and potatoes--* of this message later this week. In the meantime, via the Messages For Our Daughters facebook page (https://www.facebook.com/AuthorShonakikiP) I would love to hear from you after having read the first portion of this week's message. Even if you have to leave your message or comment anonymously by sending a private message, I'd love it if you could take the time and tell us if you've been tempted and if you were victorious in that battle. Your message will be shared with no name attached for the purpose of continuing the conversation and for support. Also, I'd love to hear why (those of you who have already done so) you date or feel the need to date.

If you do not read it all at once, in two days begin reading Part II.

WEEK 8
PART II

Now that you've had some time to ponder the question that was posed to you earlier, let us dive into the meat and potatoes of this message. There will always be consequences for the choices we make and to be quite frank with you half of the problems that young girls are faced with nowadays all have a common denominator…a boy. Wouldn't you agree? So with that said, let's talk a bit about how boys should fit into your lives. Many of you don't know what the purpose of dating is for and I assure you there is a true reason. Because you lack the knowledge of knowing what that reason is you open yourself up to unknown selfish behaviors from boys that cause you unnecessary stress and heartache in your youth. --*and those behaviors are some of the worst kind--*

Listen, my loves when you allow a guy the ***privilege*** of courting you it should be for the sole purpose of the two of you getting to know one another because he sees you as a young lady suitable to be his wife. Getting familiar with each other mentally is what will eventually be the underlying blanket of unconditional love that will help your marriage -- *should the two of you take a stroll down the aisle* -- stand through the test of times. Courting is what you do in preparation of marriage. As a Queen of 3 young ladies myself, the term courting sounds so much better than the term dating. Not to mention from where I sit it seems to diminish the connection of the whole idea of the need to have sex with the person you are familiarizing yourself with. So say it with me…Courting…Courting...C.O.U.R.T.I.N.G. --*definitely has a nice ring to it—*

When a young man who's on the right path chooses to court you it would not be in his character to ever devalue you. He will not beg of you to give yourself away undeservingly because he will understand what is at stake…your purity. Did you notice I did not say he will not ask of you? I said he will not beg of you. I did not say he would never ask because we all wrestle with the flesh at times. My integrity as a mother will not allow me to distort reality and say that a young man would never ask because just as you and I get weak at times, so shall he. However, where he is made weak for that moment I say to you it is just cause and very necessary that you adjust your princess crown. Cloak up with the strength of a lioness. Let your eyes speak in boldness as they find his in that particular moment. Be firm yet gentle with your words. Do not be afraid to share with him the youthful wisdom you've learned along the way about saving yourself for your husband.

Help him to understand that he is battling with the combination of a lustful heart and hormones. *--a battle not uncommon--* Scripture tells us ***"No temptation has overtaken you that is not common to man. God is faithful, and he will not let you be tempted beyond your ability, but with the temptation he will also provide the way of escape, that you may be able to endure it." 1* Corinthians 10:3** This scripture reminds us that God will always give us a way out if we are tempted. You just have to take it. Think of yourself as his way out. Think of yourself as the Supergirl who saved him from the sin of fornicating. If he asks, give him the way out. Scripture also reminds us that we are never tempted by things that are unknown, unheard of, or uncommon. Therefore, it will be okay for you to remind the young guys' of this should the need arise. Any young man who is worthy of sitting on the front porch sipping on sunshine with you for the rest of your life and being one with you will understand that.

With the endless rounds of sex being served to you on a mangled platter by the media, we understand the battle you all face today. My loves…we get it. What I want you to know is they have managed to taint the very thing that God has purposed to be so wonderful and amazing. Intimacy…Love…One…Marriage…Bonds…Vows…Sex; They all sound so divine as they echo one another don't they? The truth about sex is that it is one of the most delicate languages spoken between a husband and a wife. This is why it should be treated as a hidden treasure until found by the one person purposed to find it. It is meant to connect the souls on a level much deeper than you should have with anyone else other than your husband. Can you imagine what it would feel like if your husband was the only soul ever to walk the earth that knew *you*, completely? He would be the only man who could reach deep into your soul and wrap it in a love so amazing that no other man could ever pierce it. Save yourselves my darlings. Save yourselves for the man God has destined for you. Please do not dance with the idea of sharing your special gift with any young man until you have married your King. For if you do, you run the risk of tying your soul to someone else forever, and ever, and ever.

Soul Ties, you say? Why yes. Yes, there is such a thing as soul ties. In Ephesians 5:31 it says ***"For this cause shall a man leave his father***

and mother, and shall be joined unto his wife, and they two shall be one flesh." When man and woman are married, this is when they become intimate with one another in a Godly way. They become one. Ask any woman you trust to be truthful to you. Ask them if they feel differently about the guy they courted and never got intimate with and the guy they decided to have sex with. While they may have moved on happily in life and fallen in love with someone else there will always be that connection with the guy whom they've let know them inwardly. What if there is more than one? There is truly a connection that takes place. I cannot stress it enough to you. So for those of you who have not yet gone ahead and answered to your curiosity when it came knocking with this matter in hand, I say to you please wait. Hold on to your precious God given jewels for dear life and allow no one to force you to relinquish them.

For those of you that have already tip toed on the edge of fornication for the sake of wanting to be loved it is not too late for you. God forgives us for our sins. He wipes us clean and makes us anew. You can make a vow this day and repent of your sins. When He forgives you, then you be sure to forgive yourself. Once it is done, you stand up, hold your head high, and continue your journey through life moving forward. It is ok if you stumble along the way just make sure you never move backwards. Take your time and get to know you by getting to know God and when the young man who does not yet know he is destined to be your king approaches you, you will know it.

Week 8 Challenge:

1. Take this time and write a promise letter to God and yourself. Make a vow this day promising to protect your temple (body) and to preserve your purity. Whatever has come to lay on your heart significantly since you have been on this self-evaluation journey, tell God about it. Once you have completed your letter, fold it and staple it to the middle of the blank space below for safe keeping.

Be Healed by God's Love

WEEK 9

"Come now, let us settle the matter, says the Lord. Though your sins are like scarlet, they shall be white as snow; though they are red as crimson, they shall be like wool."

Isaiah 1:18 NIV

Daughters, sometimes we as mothers don't always get it right. I'm sure there may be some of you reading this and you were born to a mother who has not taught you how to properly wear your crown. She has yet to show you how to care for your crown. Because of her shortcomings, you don't know how to share love. You don't yet understand the depth of your title…future Queen. Forgive her for she is probably fighting a personal battle that not even she is yet aware of. She is not perfect neither is she exempt from making mistakes. There may be some of you who were born to a mother that worked in every way possible to add unto you all of the things she knows are within the makings of a Queen and you rebel. Remember, we are all human and we make mistakes. There is no one perfect person. Jesus is the only perfect one that has ever walked this earth.

However, here is what is beautiful about his existence in relation to you. Jesus died for our sins; your sins. In this lifetime you are sure to make mistakes. You may make some that carry with them a burden so heavy that they could cause you to doubt the wonderful mercies of God. Beloveds no matter what sinful things you may have done, it is not too late for you to start anew. Dig in to God's word and allow your spirit to curl up next to his presence. Allow yourself to be healed by HIS love. Please hear and receive this *ever so repeated* yet fabulous truth. As long as you have breath in your body HE is giving you a chance to refine your life. Don't think of it as change because let's be honest, the majority of people are hesitant when it comes to the notion of changing. However, everyone absolutely loves the idea of being refined. Does not that sound better to you?

Therefore I submit to you to seek to gain a relationship with God for yourself; for it is only then that your eyes will be unshielded to the things that should not be but opened to the things that should be. There are some of you young ladies who are reading this message and thinking about how much you have sinned already. You may be thinking it's too late and there's no hope. With God there is always hope. *As long as He allows you to awaken daily, there hope and forgiveness will always be greeting you as the day breaks*. Choose it. Choose hope. Accept that you are forgiven. Once you connect with God He will wash away all of your sins giving you another chance at being whole and pure again. Please do not become a slave to your sins. There is absolutely nothing in this world that is worth losing your mental and spiritual freedom over. Give your troubles and past sins to God and allow Him to work things out in your favor for his glory.

As you journey through this life always keep in mind, my loves, that God is forgiving. HE is merciful and HE is just. It is because of God that you could never be bound to your wrong doings provided you sincerely ask for forgiveness for whatever that sin is. These questions I pose to you. If your brother or sister pushed you down and you fell in a way that caused you to break your arm, without them asking would you forgive them? If you had a major disagreement with your best friend and he or she called you all sorts of horrible names during the argument would you forgive them? If you said yes it is probably safe to say to say that you have love for the one you forgave and there are very little wrongs they could do to you that would make you not forgive them. Now multiply your love and forgiveness times infinity. That is a mere glimpse of what God's love and HIS forgiveness for you is.

So again, I say to you seek Him in prayer. With all of your heart search for Him for with him comes an unconditional love that ceases to exist anywhere in this world. Go to Him in prayer and confess your sins. Don't be afraid to ask Him for forgiveness.--*while you're at it*-- Thank Him for covering you and keeping his hand on you even when you didn't think you deserved it. When you finish your heart to heart conversation with Him (prayer), open your eyes and see life for the first time again. For when you see life around you after you've experienced

Christ's love you will find it to be quite joyful, quite loving, and most adventurous despite all the evil in the world.

Week 9 Challenge:

This week's challenge may be the hardest one yet. Allow Jesus into your heart and give Him all of you. Repent and be baptized if you have not done so since finding Christ. Many of you may have already been baptized after coming to know Christ. If so, take this time and remember all of the reasons why you made that decision to do so. Some of you may be saying you were already baptized as a child. To that I must say, as a child you were more than likely baptized because it is what your parents wanted. To be baptized now because you have come to understand the importance of seeking to gain a personal relationship with Christ is more significant than your baptism as a child could ever be.

Journal your week 9 thoughts on the following page.

Weekly Chronicle:

_____

_____

_____

_____

_____

_____

_____

#SelfiE-VAL   #QueensBE

Forgiveness

WEEK 10

"Love is patient, love is kind. It does not envy, it does not boast, it is not proud. It does not dishonor others, it is not self-seeking, it is not easily angered, it keeps no record of wrongs. Love does not delight in evil but rejoices with the truth. "

1 Corinthians 13:4-6 NIV

It is currently 1:15 a.m. on a quiet Wednesday morning in West Virginia. After a very long day of work, I had no idea I would be up past my bedtime to greet midnight. I just picked my girls up off of the floor after they spent their evening lying around watching family shows all day and helped them settle into bed. As much as I wanted to rest my weary head it seemed so many things were tugging at me to pick up my little black notebook and write. In my ears right now is the sweet melody of Lay Me Down by Sam Smith. I have been trying to wait and allow the right message to come to me before I write to you the last message of this book. For the past few days "Forgiveness" has been laying on my heart, still. So at this very moment and time as I sit in our most comfortable, rocking recliner next to my girls as they sleep in the quiet of the night I give to you a simple message of my current thoughts on "Forgiveness".

It is more for the releasing of the unpleasant bondage that cages the most beautiful parts of your beautiful spirit. Forgiveness is truly the cure for the vengeful heart. It is the converter of hate. Though many have yet to learn this, forgiveness is like tiny specs of renewed life that lives within each and every one of you. At no time should you allow your borrowed time here on earth come to an end without sharing your spirit of forgiveness with the world. I can not tell you that the issues you deal with at your very youthful age are nothing and that it should be quite easy to forgive. Why? I can not tell you these things because I have

43

been right where you are today. No one could tell me my hurt did not matter and was not relevant. My feelings did not come with a switch designed to turn off my pain whenever I no longer wanted to feel it. Therefore I am saying to you today whatever you are going through allow God to hold your hand and keep moving forward. Let HIS love for you serve as the lantern that will guide you through when your path gets foggy. When you allow HIM to bandage your bruises and heal your heart you will find it a lot easier to forgive others of their transgressions against you.

Here is a little secret about me. When I stopped denying my anger and allowed God to move within me, I forgave. When I forgave I moved to a higher level in my walk with Christ. You must know my loves, whether it is hate in your heart or joy, the perspective of your world is shaped. Do not waste another second of your life holding on to a grudge. A grudge will most certainly stunt your growth. It will take root in your spirit and eventually bring forth rotten fruits of stubbornness and hate. 99% of you reading these messages I do not know and have never met before but I look at my daughters in this mess of a world today and my heart aches for you all. I want you all to be game changers. Stop the madness of the world with all of our beautiful queens in the making. Be the forces that shift the thoughts of all the unbelievers. Show them that you are not yet lost. Starting today I would have you to stand taller than the tallest version of you. Walk with your head held high only looking down to see who'll need your help to get back up. Be bold in speech but meek in the tone of your voice. Get to know and love all parts of you that God blessed you with. In your actions, practice daily being the queen you are destined to be. Understand that there is a reason *you were crowned at birth*. So today, right here and now make your presence known. Draw the world in with all of your unique glory then REIGN new life in it.

Are you currently holding the better parts of someone's character hostage because you are angered by their previous actions? If you find that you are fighting kinder parts of your heart because you refuse to see this person in a better light, stop now and grow. Grow. GROW.

~Reign Queens Reign~

Final Challenge: Week 10

1. Fill in the blank spaces on the following page with a list of the people you feel you need to forgive or their actions that wronged you.

   a. I am angry about
_____ but if God
comes back tomorrow will it help get me into heaven or will it
contribute to me going to hell?
   b. I am angry about
_____ but if God
comes back tomorrow will it help get me into heaven or will it
contribute to me going to hell?
   c. I am angry about
_____ but if God
comes back tomorrow will it help get me into heaven or will it
contribute to me going to hell?
   d. I am angry about
_____ but if God
comes back tomorrow will it help get me into heaven or will it
contribute to me going to hell?
   e. I am angry about
_____ but if God
comes back tomorrow will it help get me into heaven or will it
contribute to me going to hell?

Each day this week I would have you to focus on the-*what if*. What if tomorrow is the day the Lord comes back? Which road will the matters of my heart give me the right to take? Heaven or Hell?

2. Take a selfie of the newest version of you! Save it. Review all selfies and journals from the last 10 weeks.

3. Remember those little notes from week one? Have the same individuals who wrote those do the same activity again. Now compare both sets. Tell me. What do you see? Do you see a change between week one and week 10?

4. Challenge someone else with the 10 Week SelfiEVal challenge!

Last Weekly Chronicle!

#SelfiE-VAL

wQueensBE

_____

_____

_____

_____

_____

Congratulations to you for finishing your **#SelfiEVAL** journey!

About the Author

Shonakiki P. was born and raised in a small town called Camden Alabama. She ventured out into the world at the tender age of 19 and joined the United States Marine Corps. She went on to reside in numerous places, some she'd never dreamed of living in such as Japan, Hawaii, and California in particular. It would be within each of these places and others she would meet and experience beautiful people; those gripping encounters would lead her to strengthening her walk with Christ. She has now blissfully entered into yet another chapter of life which lends a platform to share her gift as an Author with the world.

Shonakiki holds degrees in Management and also Business Administration focusing on Entrepreneurial Studies from Hawaii Pacific University. She holds a Master of Arts Degree in Human Resource Management from National University in Southern California. She now resides on the east coast with her husband Larry and their children. They have three beautiful daughters, April, Laryssa, and Layla.